# ShuHaR

# FLEX FIST
# BOXING

# CODE OF THE

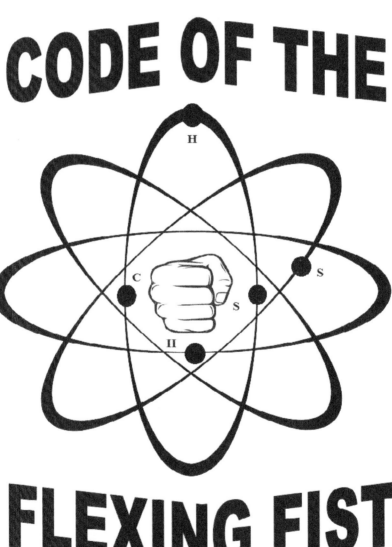

# FLEXING FIST

**By Sifu Gary Harris**

# Table of Contents

# A Message from Sifu G.

Thank you for your interest in Shu Ha Ri Do martial arts concepts. I created the Shu Ha Ri Do martial arts system in 1998. I have had hundreds of students since that time. Shu Ha Ri Do is a complete martial arts system that covers all ranges of combat from self-defense, boxing, kickboxing, and ground-fighting, even animalistic forms. Flex Fist boxing is just one of the many signature concepts found within Shu Ha Ri Do. Flex Fist boxing is not a replacement for "conventional boxing" (jab, cross, hook, etc.) which is also a part of Shu Ha Ri Do training. When you see the hand open before impact think of it like this, water turning to ice, the open hand is water, and the closed fist is ice. Closing or "flexing" the fist and arm muscles upon impact add snap and explosion without telegraphing. Feel free to look for my other books. To all of my students current and former I thank you for your dedication to self-mastery physically, mentally and spiritually. Continue with the Shu Ha Ri Do Code of "Wisdom Before Combat" Osu!

## www.shuharido.com

# Flex Fist Q & A

**Q.** What is Flex Fist boxing

**A.** Flex Fist boxing is a boxing concept originated by Sifu G. J. Harris that emphasizes, speed, power, non-telegraphed motions, and progressively complex combinations.

**Q.** Why is it called Flex Fist?

**A.** It is called Flex Fist because, a big part of the power and speed is derived from flexing the fist and arm muscles at the moment of impact.

**Q.** Why are hands open and not making a fist before you punch.

**A.** With Shu Ha Ri Do Flex Fist boxing the focus is on maximizing speed, power, with non-telegraphed motions. Closing the fist upon impact increases speed, and power. However, closing the fist upon impact should not be viewed universally. There are times when it may be useful to some to keep the fists closed before impact, it depends on the person and the scenario.

CODE OF THE THE BACKBONE OF SURPRISE IS FUSING SPEED WITH SECRECY

FLEXING FIST

FLEX FIST BOXING

WWW.SHUHARIDO.COM

# Flex Fist Boxing Introduction

Shu Ha Ri Do Flex Fist Boxing consists of 7 fundamentals of speed. They are 1.Spinning 2.Hinge 3.Hammer 4.Closing 5.Swivel 6.Hanging and 7.Pulling fists. These fundamentals are based on striking without telegraphing or any wasted motion. Shu Ha Ri Do Flex Fist Boxing utilizes the Centerline Principle. Picture a line drawn down the middle of your opponent, now focus your strikes on that line. This philosophy makes you mechanically faster. There are exceptions to the Centerline Principle, such as with the Shu Ha Ri Do Swivel Hook. You will see more about the Swivel Hook in the following pages. Using these fundamentals, anyone can become faster with their hands. These fundamentals are not based on fast twitch muscle fibers, but mechanics! Master the mechanics and speed becomes elementary. The 7 fundamentals of speed I present to you are cutting edge in their application, thank you for reading.

## STANCES

This is the Man Sau position. To develop explosive power practice your Flex Fist punches from this stance. DO NOT turn your shoulders, torso, or waist when punching. Instead generate all of the power you put into your punches from the ground and your core. Explode forward flexing each punch and your core.

## STANCE 2

This is the fighting position/stance. Unlike the Man Sau position where you do not turn the shoulder, obviously you turn the shoulder in this stance. If you get thousands of punch repetitions in the Man Sau position and learn to generate great power without turning your shoulder, imagine how much more powerful your punches will become when do turn your shoulder!

# Spinning Fist

The fundamentals of speed that will be introduced in the upcoming pages are based on non-telegraphed precise motions. Let's start with the Shu Ha Ri Do Spinning Fist. How the Spinning Fist displays precision and non-telegraphed motions is by spinning forward, borrowing into the target. The centrifugal force generated by this motion results in speed, power and damage with nearly no shoulder movement at all. Shoulder movement is one of the key indicators that a strike could be coming.

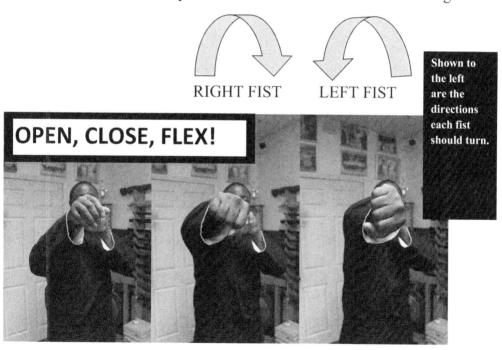

RIGHT FIST    LEFT FIST

**Shown to the left are the directions each fist should turn.**

**OPEN, CLOSE, FLEX!**

# Spinning Fist Application

By "splitting the gap" or using a simple parry or slip block you can strike your opponent by surprise.

## *Spinning Fist Illustration*

When executing the spinning fist technique imagine your fist as a screw, and your arm as the screw driver.

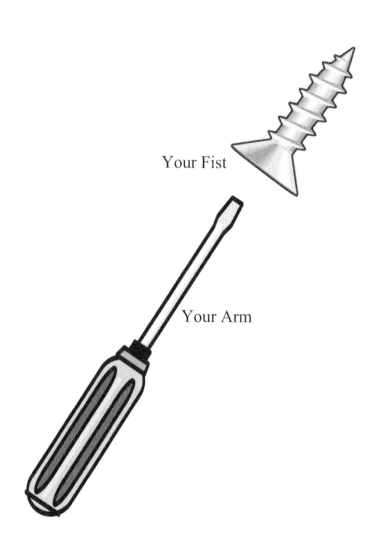

Your Fist

Your Arm

# Hinge Fist

The Shu Ha Ri Do Hinge Fist can best be understood by visualizing a door swinging open rapidly. The Flex Fist concept can readily be seen as the fist, forearm, and triceps are flexed when hitting the target. Now the pulling fist concept for hinge fist can be understood by visualizing a door closing rapidly.

OPEN, CLOSE, FLEX!

Notice the fist closing and flexing upon impact in the pictures. Flexing allows maximum power from with no extra movement or telegraphing.

OPEN, CLOSE, FLEX!

IF YOUR OPPONENT BLOCKS YOUR HINGE FIST, THEN OPEN YOUR HAND AND TRANSITION INTO A HINGE FIST LOW AS SHOWN.

## *Hinge Fist Illustration ("The Swinging Door")*

Your Fist

Your Elbow

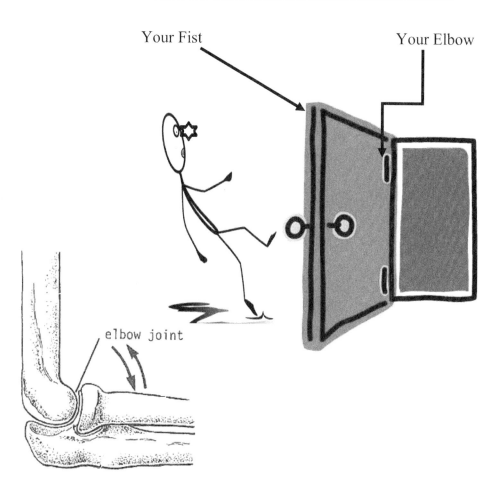

elbow joint

# Hammer Fist

The Shu Ha Ri Do Hammer Fist uses the same idea as the hinge fist only it moves downward, picture a hammer pounding a nail. In most cases the target will be the opponent's nose.

Although the Hammer Fist is not the most practical of punches. It can be readily used for certain self-defense scenarios.

## *Hammer Fist Application*

**OPEN, CLOSE, FLEX!**

# _Hammer Fist Illustration_

Simply put, when executing the hammer fist visualize the action of a hammer.

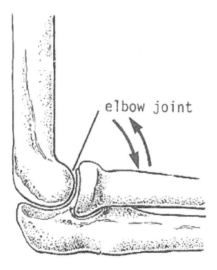

elbow joint

The Hammer Fist is an extension of the Hinge Fist fundamental.

# Closing Fist

Although, all of the punches should be done closing fist upon impact. The closing fist is perhaps the quickest of the fundamentals of speed in Flex Fist boxing. I call it "Closin Fist" primarily because of it's closing speed". From a fighting position, you simply close your fist into the target while flexing your fist, forearm and triceps muscles.

To the right are the opening and mid stages of the closing fist. Make sure fingers are fused together.

**OPEN, CLOSE, FLEX!**

Final stage of the closing fist. Your arm muscles should be flexed tightly. This adds maximum penetration to your punch.

STRIKE ON THE CENTER-LINE

# Closing fist application

Closing fist to face through the guard.

OPEN, CLOSE, FLEX!

By side stepping, or slipping you can execute a closing fist to your opponents face from the outside.

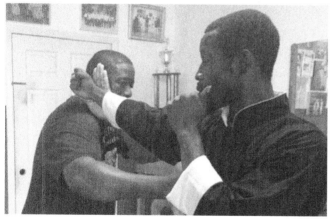
You can also execute a closing fist to the center mass of your opponent. Think of how closing and flexing upon impact increases the effect when you strike the solar plexus or stomach.

# *Closing Fist Illustration*

When executing the closing fist visualize a missile being fired into a target. Think of how the missile trajectory is as straight as an arrow it does not deviate left or right but center. Always remember the centerline principle.

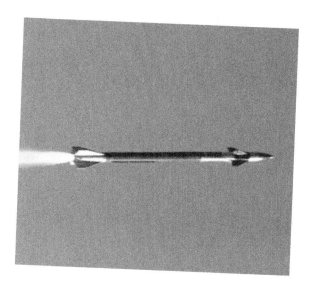

# Hanging Fist/Hand

he Shu Ha Ri Do Hanging Fist serves a dual purpose. The Hanging Fist an be used as a block as in Muay Thai, or Wing Chun, (Bong Sao) or as a transition into the Swivel Fist which you will see in the next section.

Notice how the hand/fist hangs downward. This sets the stage for a "Swivel Fist" transition which will be shown on the following pages.

# Swivel Fist

If the closing fist is the quickest strike, then the Swivel Fist would have to be the sneakiest punch taught in Shu Ha Ri Do Flex Fist boxing. The Swivel Fist moves in the same way that a curve ball in baseball does it, changes direction in midair. The Swivel Fist as will be shown in the upcoming photos will at times transit from under the opponents chin to striking the side of the head. Other times, it may move forward and switch directions again striking the side of the opponents face depending on the scenario.

## *Swivel Fist Application*

OPEN, CLOSE, FLEX!

The Swivel Hook/Fist should transition around the face or head, striking the eye, jaw, chin, or back of head, landing knuckles first.

These are pics of how to throw a lead Swivel Fist. Raising the elbow as you bring your hand forward and into a sharp turn is very important. The power of the Swivel Fist is in the tightness of the curve. Too wide of an arc causes a loss of power. Keep the circle tight by moving your hand toward the face and making a sharp turn.

**OPEN, CLOSE, FLEX!**

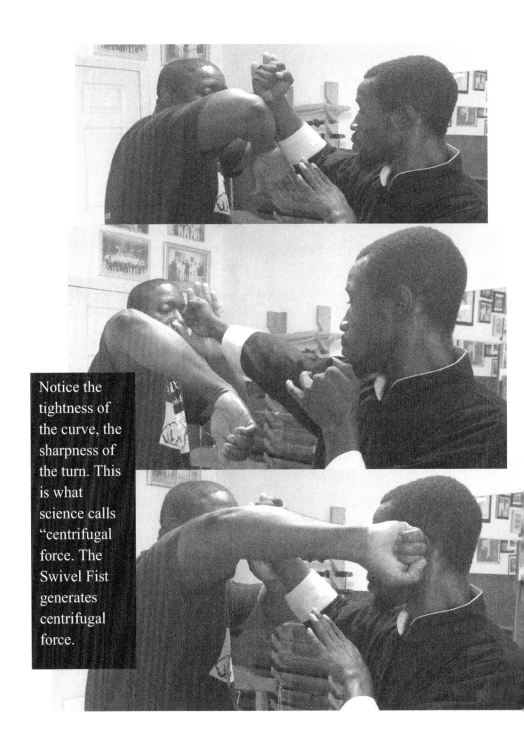

Notice the tightness of the curve, the sharpness of the turn. This is what science calls "centrifugal force. The Swivel Fist generates centrifugal force.

## *Swivel Fist Illustration*

When executing the Swivel Fist visualize the motion of a whip and how

it explodes at the tip. As soft and small as a whip is it can produce

devastating results, so it is with the Swivel Fist.

You can also visualize the Swivel Fist as you would a curveball in

baseball.

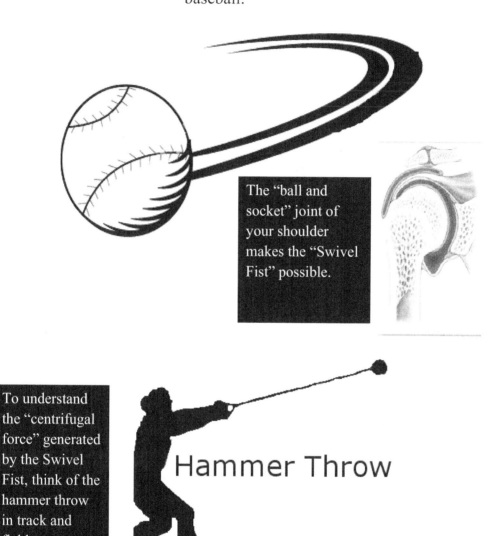

The "ball and socket" joint of your shoulder makes the "Swivel Fist" possible.

To understand the "centrifugal force" generated by the Swivel Fist, think of the hammer throw in track and field.

Hammer Throw

# FROM WATER TO ICE

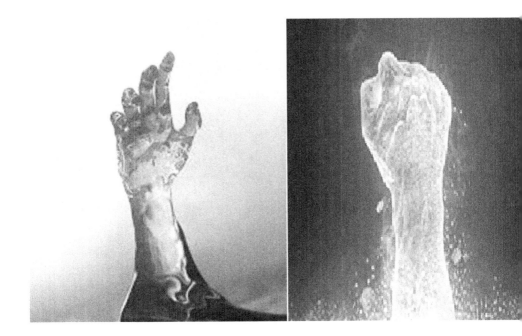

When you think of Flex Fist Boxing think of this analogy "From Water to Ice". When moving toward your target you hand will move faster when it is relaxed like water. Then right upon impact freeze your "water" by closing your fist and flexing wrist and arm muscles.

# Pulling Fist/Hand

It is important to remember the benefit of the pulling fist philosophy. The faster you pull your hand back from a punch, the faster you are able to punch again. I will not attempt to illustrate the pulling fist philosophy with photos in this book, as it would be hard to tell the difference between a pull and a strike. Since you have already seen each punch, to keep it simple think of the pulling fist this way:

**Spinning Fist:** With this punch your fist, always, rotates toward your thumb, when "pulling" it rotates toward the pinkie.

**Hinge Fist:** With this pull simply think in terms of a closing door. The same way it opens outward toward your opponent's face, it closes toward your own. However, be sure to lower the elbow as you are "closing the door".

**Hammer Fist:** With this "pull" just like the Hinge Fist, quickly return to your face on the same path as the punch was thrown.

**Closing Fist/Swivel Fist:** Once again quickly return to your face on the same path as the punch was thrown. So in essence the Swivel moves under, forward, and around. When pulling, your hand should move, around, under, and backward toward you.

This is the essence of Shu Ha Ri Do originality, and creativity. Imitation, CEATION, and lastly perfection, is the summary I use to describe the Shu Ha Ri Do (Way). Perfection is a lifetime commitment and it will never be reached, however, the pursuit of perfection will keep us busy for eternity. Hopefully, you enjoyed reading this book and found the techniques useful. If you are a fighter, or a regular citizen repeated practice of these techniques will have an immediate impact on your striking, and ability to defend yourself. Please look for my other books which you will see in the following pages. There are more books about Shu Ha Ri Do techniques coming soon, be sure to refer to www.shuharido.com often. Thank you for reading.

**WWW.SHUHARIDO.COM**

Gary Jones Harris
Author of *The Awareness Formula*

# HARNESS THE POWER
# WITHIN
# AND
# WITHOUT

Overcome Mental
and Spiritual Manipulation
Through Self Mastery

Legacy

Shu Ha Ri

# THE MOST POWERFUL POETRY YOU WILL EVER READ!

## The Book Of

# *Hai/Clae*

*Poetic nuggets of truth and inspiration for seekers of God on the path.*

Including a discourse on the deception of Pseudo Energy and Pseudo Knowledge the ultimate mind traps.

# DECIPHER UNRAVEL COMPREHEND

In your quest for truth consider the ion: An *ion* is a negatively or positively charged atom. Well no *ion* has more positive charge than the QUEST-*ion*

## Gary Jones Harris

25

Printed in Great Britain
by Amazon

55902424R10020